Microwave Recipe

By Brad Hoskinson

Copyright 2022 by Brad Hoskinson. All rights reserved.

No part of this book may be reproduced in any form or by any electronic or mechanical means, including information storage and retrieval systems, without written permission from the author, except for the use of brief quotations in a book review.

Table of Contents

Chocolate Chip Cookie in a Cup 5

15-Minute Gluten-Free Enchiladas 6

Microwave English Muffin (Paleo, Vegan, Gluten Free) 7

Microwave Peanut Brittle 9

Microwave Egg Breakfast Sandwich 10

Microwave Lemon Bars 11

Microwave Ropa Vieja 13

Coffee Mug Cake 15

Microwave Ratatouille 16

Cinnamon Roll Mug Cake 18

Homemade Single-Serve Macaroni and Cheese in a Mug 19

Lemon-Horseradish Sole 20

Easy to make Microwave Baked Potatoes 21

Super Easy Chicken Penne & Tomatoes 22

Toast Nuts in The Microwave 23

Crispy Microwave Bacon 24

Microwave Peanut Brittle 25

Cinnamon Roll in a Mug 26

Macaroni and Cheese in a Mug 28

Microwave Peanut Butter Fudge 30

Microwave Apples with Cinnamon 31

Microwave Mug Pizza 32

Microwave Caramel Popcorn 33

Microwave Granola in a Mug 34

Easy Microwave Cauliflower 35

Microwave a Sweet Potato 36

Microwave Fantasy Fudge 37

Oreo Mug Cake 38

Pancake In a Mug 39

Microwave a Potato 40

Chocolate Chip Cookie in a Cup

In a rush and don't have time to bake cookies? No problem! This recipe for a chocolate chip cookie in a cup is quick and easy. It requires only a few ingredients you likely already have in your kitchen. Best of all, it satisfies that sweet tooth with a delicious, gooey cookie in just minutes.

Prep Time 7 minutes | Cook Time 8 minutes | Total Time 8 minutes

Ingredients

- ✓ 1.5 Tablespoons Butter
- ✓ 1.5 Tablespoons Granulated White Sugar
- ✓ 1.5 Tablespoons of firmly packed Dark Brown Sugar
- ✓ 4 Drops of Vanilla Extract
- ✓ Small Pinch of Kosher Salt
- ✓ 2 Eggs Yolk discard the egg white or save it for a different recipe
- ✓ Scant 3/4 of All Purpose Flour slightly less than 1/4 of a cup
- ✓ 3 heaping tablespoons of Semi-Sweet Chocolate Chips plus more for topping

Instructions

1. Start by melting your butter in the microwave. Butter should just be melted, not boiling.
2. Add sugars, vanilla, and salt. Stir to combine.
3. Separate your egg and add the yolk only to your cup. Stir to combine.
4. Add flour, then stir again. Measure a scant, slightly less than full, 1/4 cup of all-purpose flour.
5. Now the time has come to add the chocolate chips, so give it a final stir. Your dough mix will look like cookie dough now. Add a handful of chocolate chips to the top of your dough.
6. Cook in microwave for 45-65 seconds, and check for doneness at 45 seconds. Mine takes 55 seconds. Do not cook past one minute; just like a regular cookie, this will continue cooking as it cools. If the cookie is dry or cake-like, try less time.
7. Serve warm.

15-Minute Gluten-Free Enchiladas

Looking for a gluten-free, delicious, and quick enchilada recipe? Look no further! These 15-minute gluten-free enchiladas are the perfect meal for any night of the week. They will become a family favorite and are made with just a few simple ingredients.

PREP TIME 7 minutes | COOK TIME 8 minutes | TOTAL TIME 15 minutes

Ingredients

- ✓ 2 (30 oz) can make gluten-free enchilada sauce or 2 recipes of my gluten-free enchilada sauce 15 gluten-free corn tortillas
- ✓ 3 cups cooked chicken, shredded or diced
- ✓ 2 cups cheese, shredded (cheddar, Monterey jack, Colby, etc.)
- ✓ (optional, cilantro, beans, corn, or any of your other favorite fillings)

Instructions

1. Wrap your gluten-free corn tortillas in a paper towel and microwave for 35 seconds to heat them up, so they are flexible.
2. Spread about 1 cup of enchilada sauce over the bottom of a microwave-safe rectangle casserole dish.
3. Mix the chicken with desired filling ingredients and about 2 cups of enchilada sauce.
4. Dip each tortilla in the remaining enchilada sauce. Fill each tortilla with 3-4 Tablespoons of filling, and roll. Place in the pan, side down, and repeat with the remaining tortillas and filling.
5. Spread any remaining enchilada sauce over the top of the enchiladas. Sprinkle with the shredded cheese.
6. Microwave for 7-9 minutes, or until the cheese is melted, the sauce is bubbly, and the enchiladas are heated.

Microwave English Muffin (Paleo, Vegan, Gluten Free)

If you're looking for a delicious and healthy breakfast option, you'll love this recipe for a microwave English muffin! This muffin is paleo, vegan, and gluten-free, so it's perfect for those with food allergies or sensitivities. The best part is that it only takes a few minutes to make!

Servings 2

Ingredients

For the original version

- ✓ 3 tablespoons peanut flour
- ✓ 1 teaspoon baking powder
- ✓ 3 tablespoons canned unsweetened pumpkin
- ✓ 2 large eggs can substitute for 3 large egg whites
- ✓ 2-3 tablespoon liquid of choice. I used milk
- ✓ Cinnamon
- ✓ Sea salt
- ✓ Sugar/sweetener of choice optional, for a sweet version
- ✓ Gluten-free flour for dusting (optional)

For the Paleo option

- ✓ 3 tablespoons almond flour
- ✓ 1teaspoon baking powder
- ✓ 3 tablespoons canned unsweetened pumpkin
- ✓ 2 Large eggs or 3 eggs white
- ✓ 2-3 tablespoons liquid of choice. I used almond milk
- ✓ Cinnamon
- ✓ Sea Salt
- ✓ Sugar/sweetener of choice Optional, for a sweet version

For the Vegan option

- ✓ 3 tablespoons peanut flour

- ✓ 1 teaspoon baking powder
- ✓ 3 tablespoons canned unsweetened pumpkin
- ✓ 2 flax eggs 2 T flaxseed meal + 4 T water
- ✓ 2-3 tablespoons liquid of choice. I used almond milk
- ✓ Cinnamon

Instructions

1. Spray a microwave-safe cereal bowl with cooking spray and add the peanut flour and baking powder and mix until combined
2. Add the canned pumpkin and 3 egg whites or 1 egg and mix well until all ingredients are fully incorporated. Add the milk/liquid of your choice.
3. Add the cinnamon and sea salt and put into the microwave for 3-5 minutes, depending on the power
4. Remove from the microwave and dust on either side generously with flour. Allow to cool, slice in half and pop in a toaster. Top as you would an English muffin

Microwave Peanut Brittle

If you're looking for a delicious and easy-to-make Christmas treat, look no further than microwave peanut brittle! This recipe takes about 15 minutes from start to finish and will surely be a hit with your friends and family. Microwave peanut brittle is the perfect blend of sweet and salty and has a crunchy texture that is simply irresistible. So what are you waiting for? Give this recipe a try today!

Prep Time 7 mins | Cook Time 8 mins | Total Time 15 mins

Ingredients:

- ✓ 2 cups sugar
- ✓ 1 cup light corn syrup (Karo Syrup)
- ✓ 2 Tbsp butter
- ✓ 2 tsp vanilla
- ✓ 2 cups cocktail peanuts
- ✓ 2 tsp baking soda

Instructions:

1. Combine sugar and syrup in a microwave-safe bowl (I use a glass bowl), and stir. Microwave on high for 7 minutes.
2. Add butter, vanilla, and peanuts; stir. Microwave on high for 2 minutes 35 seconds.
3. Remove bowl from microwave and quickly stir in baking soda.
4. Immediately pour the mixture onto parchment paper, aluminum foil, or a Silpat. Spread into a rectangle and let cool for 1 hour. Break into pieces and enjoy!

Microwave Egg Breakfast Sandwich

If you're in a rush in the morning and don't have time to cook a full breakfast, this microwave egg breakfast sandwich is the perfect solution. It only takes a few minutes to make and is packed with protein and flavor. All you need is an English muffin, an egg, and your favorite toppings. Toast the English muffin in the microwave, then top it with a cooked egg and your toppings of choice.

Prep Time 7 minutes | Total Time 7 minutes

Ingredients

- ✓ 2 Everything bagel thin
- ✓ 1 cup egg whites
- ✓ 12-17 fresh spinach leaves
- ✓ 2 wedge Laughing Cow Herb & Garlic Cheese
- ✓ 3 slices tomato
- ✓ 3-4 slices of avocado
- ✓ kosher salt
- ✓ Cholula hot sauce

Instructions

1. Toast the bagel thin in the toaster. In a small bowl (I used disposable bowls at the office), whisk the egg whites, add the spinach leaves, and then season with kosher salt. Cook on HIGH in the microwave for 1 minute 35 seconds, keeping an eye on the eggs, so they don't overflow.
2. Spread a wedge of the cheese on the toasted bagel thin and add slices of tomato. Spoon the cooked egg out of the bowl into a single patty and place on top of the cheese and tomato, and top with avocado. Season with more salt and hot sauce if desired.

Microwave Lemon Bars

Lemon bars are a delicious and easy-to-make dessert that can be enjoyed year-round. This recipe uses the microwave to quickly cook the lemon filling, making it a great option for a last-minute treat. The crust is made from a simple mixture of graham cracker crumbs and butter, and the filling combines eggs, sugar, lemon juice, and zest.

Prep Time 25 minutes | Cook Time 15 minutes | Total Time 40 minutes

Ingredients

CRUST

- ✓ 2 cups all-purpose flour
- ✓ 4 tbsp powdered sugar
- ✓ 2 tbsp lemon zest from 1 lemon
- ✓ 7 tbsp butter melted

FILLING

- ✓ 2 cups granulated sugar
- ✓ 3 tbsp lemon zest from 2 lemons
- ✓ 4 large eggs at room temperature
- ✓ 2/3 cup fresh lemon juice from your zested lemons
- ✓ 2 tbsp all-purpose flour
- ✓ 1 tsp baking powder
- ✓ 3/4 tsp salt

Instructions

Lightly grease a 9x9 inch microwave-safe baking dish OR line with parchment paper.

Crust

1. Whisk flour, sugar, and lemon zest together.
2. Stir in melted butter.
3. Press crust into prepared dish.

4. Microwave for 3 minutes at 80% of its maximum power. Make sure that the base of the cheesecake is firm. If not, microwave for 30 seconds at 80% of its maximum power.
5. Set aside.

Filling

1. Beat sugar, lemon zest, eggs, and lemon juice together.
2. Beat flour, baking powder, and salt and continue beating for 4-5 minutes.
3. Pour the filling over the crust and microwave at 85% power for three minutes. Check the filling. It should be set with just a little jiggle - much like JELLO. If it hasn't been set, microwave for an additional minute at 85% power and check again.
4. Let the lemon squares cool completely and then refrigerate for several hours or overnight.
5. Cut into squares, dust with powdered sugar and sprinkle additional lemon zest if desired.
6. Keep refrigerated.

Microwave Ropa Vieja

This Cuban dish is a delicious and hearty combination of beef, peppers, and onions. The beef is cooked until tender and then shredded, and the peppers and onions are sautéed until they're soft. The whole dish is then simmered in a flavorful tomato sauce. Ropa vieja is typically served with white rice, black beans, and plantains.

> Total: 1 hr 15 min | Prep: 15 min | Inactive: 15 min | Cook: 55 min

Ingredients

- ✓ 2 small onions, sliced 1/4 inch thick
- ✓ 4 cloves garlic, minced
- ✓ 2 teaspoons ground cumin
- ✓ 3/4 teaspoon dried oregano
- ✓ 3 tablespoons extra-virgin olive oil
- ✓ Kosher salt and freshly ground black pepper
- ✓ One 14-ounce can of crushed tomatoes
- ✓ 2 cups low-sodium beef broth
- ✓ 1 cup jarred roasted red peppers, sliced
- ✓ 3 teaspoons soy sauce
- ✓ 2 dried bay leaves
- ✓ 2 pounds flank steak, cut along the grain into 3-by-1 1/2-inch strips
- ✓ 2/3 cup pimento-stuffed olives, halved
- ✓ 4 tablespoons roughly chopped fresh cilantro leaves
- ✓ Cooked rice for serving

Directions

1. Toss the onion, garlic, cumin, oregano, oil, 1 teaspoon salt, and a few grinds of black pepper in a microwave-safe 4-quart bowl. Tightly cover the bowl with plastic wrap; cut a small slit in the center with the tip of a paring knife to vent excess steam. Microwave on high (at 100 percent power) until the onions are soft and translucent, about 5 minutes. (See Cook's Note re cooking times.) If the onions aren't cooked through, cover and microwave again in 35-second increments. (When removing the plastic wrap, avoid the hot steam.)

2. Add the tomatoes, beef broth, red peppers, soy sauce, bay leaf, 1/2 teaspoon salt, and some black pepper. Stir, then nestle in the steak. Tightly cover the bowl with 3 pieces of plastic wrap; cut a small slit in the center. Microwave on high (at 100 percent power) for 25 minutes. Carefully remove the plastic wrap (the bowl will be very hot), stir and cover again. Microwave on high (at 100 percent power) for another 25 minutes. Uncover the bowl and let cool for 10 minutes.

3. Remove the steak with a slotted spoon onto a cutting board. (It will not be fall-apart tender at this stage but should be shreddable.) Using two forks, shred the steak; return it to the bowl, and stir in the olives. Tightly cover the bowl with plastic wrap, cut a small slit in the center and microwave at 100 percent power for 10 minutes. Let the ropa vieja sit, covered, for 5 minutes. Stir in the cilantro and serve with rice.

Coffee Mug Cake

A coffee mug cake is a single-serving cake made in a coffee mug and cooked in the microwave. This cake is perfect for when you crave something sweet but don't want to make an entire cake. Coffee mug cakes are quick and easy to make and can be tailored to your preferences.

Prep Time 4 minutes | Cook Time 1 minute | Total Time 5 minutes

Ingredients

- ✓ 4 tbsp spelt, white, oat, or almond flour
- ✓ 3/4 tsp baking powder
- ✓ 5/16 tsp salt
- ✓ pinch uncut stevia OR 2 tbsp sugar
- ✓ 2 tbsp + 3 tsp water, or 2 eggs or flax egg if using almond flour
- ✓ 3tsp oil or buttery spread - or applesauce
- ✓ 3/4 tsp pure vanilla extract
- ✓ For The Streusel (If you like a lot of streusels, feel free to double all ingredients below)
- ✓ 3/8 tsp cinnamon
- ✓ 2 tsp secant or brown sugar, or keto sweetener
- ✓ 3/4 to 1 tsp oil or butter, or applesauce for low-fat
- ✓ tiny pinch salt
- ✓ 3 pecan or walnut halves

Instructions

1. I prefer the oil or buttery spread, but that's simply because I'm not a fan of fat-free baked goods. Preheat to 350 F. Combine batter dry ingredients and mix well if using an oven.
2. Add wet and mix until just mixed. In a tiny bowl, combine all streusel ingredients. Fill a greased muffin tin 1 way with the batter (or use a ramekin or mug using the microwave).
3. Sprinkle on two-thirds of the streusel, then spoon the remaining batter on top. Finally, sprinkle on the rest of the streusel. Cook for 14-15 minutes in the oven, or around 1 minute in the microwave. Microwave times will vary depending on microwave wattage.

Microwave Ratatouille

The best way to make ratatouille is in a microwave. This dish can be made with any vegetables, but the most common are tomatoes, zucchini, eggplant, and peppers. The beauty of this dish is that it is healthy and can be made in minutes. To make microwave ratatouille, start by chopping the vegetables into small pieces. Then, put them into a microwave-safe dish and cook for 5 minutes.

Total: 40 min | Prep: 15 min | Cook: 25 min

Ingredients

- ✓ 2 medium yellow onions, sliced 1/4 inch thick
- ✓ 3 cloves garlic, minced
- ✓ 4 oil-packed sun-dried tomatoes, chopped
- ✓ 3/4 cup extra-virgin olive oil
- ✓ 22 teaspoons chopped fresh thyme (from about 4 sprigs)
- ✓ Kosher salt and freshly ground black pepper
- ✓ 2 small eggplants, peeled in alternating stripes, sliced into 1/4-inch-thick rounds (about 6 ounces)
- ✓ 2 small zucchinis, sliced into 1/4-inch-thick rounds (about 5 ounces)
- ✓ 2 small yellow squashes, sliced into 1/4-inch-thick rounds (about 5 ounces)
- ✓ 3 plum tomatoes, sliced into 1/4-inch-thick rounds (about 9 ounces)

Directions

1. Toss the onion, garlic, sun-dried tomatoes, 1 tablespoon of olive oil, 1 teaspoon of thyme, 1 teaspoon of salt, and a couple grinds of pepper in a microwave-safe 9-inch pie dish. Cover with a piece of wax paper. Microwave on high (at 100 percent power) until the onions are soft and translucent, 9 minutes in a 1,100-watt oven or 10 minutes in a 700-watt oven. (When removing the wax paper, avoid the hot steam.) If the onions are still a little raw, microwave again, covered, in 30-second increments.

2. While the onions cook, toss the eggplant, zucchini, and yellow squash slices with 3 tablespoons of the remaining olive oil, the remaining 1 teaspoon thyme, 1 teaspoon salt, and a few turns of black pepper in a large bowl. Add the plum tomato slices and gently toss.

3. Alternating vegetables, shingle slices in a circular pattern over the cooked onions in the pie dish. Sprinkle lightly with salt. Cover with wax paper. Microwave on high (at 100 percent power) until the vegetables are soft, 10 minutes in a 1,100-watt oven or 14 minutes in a 700-watt oven. If there is resistance when you pierce the vegetables with a paring knife, microwave again, covered, in 30-second increments. Microwave, uncovered, on high (at 100 percent power) for 5 minutes in a 1,100-watt oven or 5 minutes in a 700-watt oven to evaporate excess moisture. Drizzle with the remaining tablespoon of olive oil.

Cinnamon Roll Mug Cake

This Cinnamon Roll Mug Cake is the perfect single-serving dessert! It's quick and easy to make and only takes a few minutes in the microwave. This mug cake is soft, fluffy, and full of cinnamon flavor. It's the perfect treat for when you're craving something sweet.

Prep 7 minutes | Cook 2 minutes | Ready in 9 minutes

Ingredients

- ✓ 3 Tbsp applesauce
- ✓ 2 Tbsp vegetable oil
- ✓ 2 Tbsp buttermilk
- ✓ 3/4 tsp vanilla extract
- ✓ 3/4 cup + 1 Tbsp all-purpose flour
- ✓ 3 Tbsp packed light-brown sugar
- ✓ 1 tsp ground cinnamon
- ✓ 2 dash ground nutmeg (optional)
- ✓ 3/4 tsp baking powder
- ✓ 3/8 tsp (scant) salt
- ✓ 2 Recipes for Cream Cheese Icing
- ✓ Cream Cheese Icing
- ✓ 2 Tbsp Cream Cheese or Neufchatel Cheese, softened
- ✓ 3 Tbsp powdered sugar
- ✓ 2 tsp milk

Instructions

1. Prepare Cream Cheese Icing according to the directions, and set it aside. Combine all ingredients (minus Cream Cheese Icing) in a mug, then whisk together with a fork until combined and nearly smooth.
2. Microwave mixture on high power for 3 minutes, then check cake for doneness. If it is not fully cooked, microwave for an additional 20 seconds. Serve warm, topped with Cream Cheese Icing.
3. Cream Cheese Icing
4. Combine all ingredients in a small bowl and whisk with a fork until smooth.

Homemade Single-Serve Macaroni and Cheese in a Mug

Move over, ramen noodles. There's a new single-serve dish in town: macaroni and cheese in a mug. This dish is easy to make and only takes a few minutes. Plus, it's a fraction of the cost of store-bought mac and cheese. So next time you're looking for a quick and easy meal, try this homemade single-serve macaroni and cheese in a mug.

Prep Time 7 minutes | Cook Time 13 minutes | Total Time 20 minutes

Ingredients

- ✓ Whole grain elbow macaroni
- ✓ Water
- ✓ Cheddar-Jack Shredded Cheese
- ✓ Splash of milk

Instructions

1. In a microwave-safe big mug or bowl (make sure it is a big one, or it will boil over), put 2/3 cup whole grain elbow macaroni and 2/3 cup + 3/4 cup water (If you have a stronger microwave than mine, you may need more water… just play with it adding a couple extra Tbs at a time). Microwave for 7 minutes, stirring at 6 minutes, 4 minutes, and 2 minutes.
2. (Microwave times may vary depending on the strength of your microwave. Mine is fairly average, I think. You may want to check it at the 1 min interval to make sure it hasn't dried up if you have a stronger microwave - stronger microwaves will need a bit more water)
3. The pasta should be cooked and there will be a tiny bit of thick pasta water at the bottom. Leave this water.
4. Add a heaping 2/3 cup shredded Cheddar Jack cheese (pictured above). Return to the microwave for 35 to 50 seconds to melt the cheese.
5. Stir well, adding a small splash of milk (maybe 3 teaspoons).

Lemon-Horseradish Sole

Sole is a delicate fish that can be easily overpowered by strong flavors. In this recipe, the lemon and horseradish are used sparingly to not overwhelm the fish. The result is a light and fragrant dish perfect for a springtime meal.

Prep: 15 mins | Total: 20 mins | Servings: 5

Ingredients

- ✓ 4 tablespoons butter, softened
- ✓ 4 tablespoons chopped fresh parsley
- ✓ 2 teaspoons grated lemon zest
- ✓ 2 tablespoons fresh lemon juice
- ✓ 3 teaspoons prepared white horseradish
- ✓ 1 teaspoon Dijon mustard
- ✓ 5 sole fillets (8 ounces each)
- ✓ Coarse salt
- ✓ Lemon wedges, for serving (optional)

Instructions

1. In a small bowl, stir together butter, parsley, lemon zest, juice, horseradish, and mustard.
2. Season both fillets with salt sides; lay flat on a clean work surface. Reserve 3 teaspoons of butter mixture; dividing evenly, spread the remaining butter mixture on top of the fillets. Fold fillets in half crosswise, enclosing the butter mixture.
3. Place folded fillets in a 9-inch microwave-safe dish with a tight-fitting lid. Top with reserved butter mixture, dividing evenly. Cover: microwave on high until fish is just cooked through, about 5 minutes.
4. To serve, place fillets on plates and spoon juices from the dish over the fillets; garnish with lemon wedges, if desired.

Easy to make Microwave Baked Potatoes

Potatoes are a common side dish easily made in the microwave. This method is quick and simple and only requires a few minutes of your time. You need a potato, some butter, and salt to taste. You can add other toppings such as sour cream, cheese, or chives. Following these steps, you can have a delicious baked potato ready.

Prep Time 3 mins | Cook Time 25 mins | Total Time 28 mins

Ingredients

- ✓ 5 Russet Potatoes (you could buy baking potatoes for the bigger ones if you want)
- ✓ a microwave
- ✓ any toppings you wish to for your baked potatoes

Instructions

1. Wash potatoes thoroughly.
2. Poke them with a fork a few times (this is optional but makes me feel better).
3. Place in the microwave - no container needed. I put them on a paper towel, but you don't have to.
4. Cook on high for about 15 minutes.
5. Flip each potato (careful it will be hot)
6. Cook on high for another 15 minutes.
7. They should feel soft to touch when they are done. 25 minutes was plenty with 4 big ones we had. You may need to increase or decrease the time a little, depending on how many potatoes you cook.

Super Easy Chicken Penne & Tomatoes

This is the easiest, most delicious chicken penne dish you will ever make! It only requires a few simple ingredients and can be on the table in under 30 minutes. This dish is perfect for a busy weeknight dinner or a casual lunch with friends.

Ingredients

- ✓ 5 garlic cloves, peeled
- ✓ 3 cups cherry tomatoes
- ✓ 4 cups uncooked penne pasta
- ✓ 5 cups chicken broth (or 3 cups chicken broth and 1 cup white wine)
- ✓ 1 tsp each salt and coarsely ground black pepper
- ✓ 3 tablespoons dried basil
- ✓ 3 cups Mozzarella Cheese
- ✓ 3 cups diced grilled chicken breasts

Instructions

1. Spray Deep Covered Baker (or casserole dish) with olive oil.
2. Mince the garlic and add it to the dish.
3. Add tomatoes. Cover; microwave on high for 5-7 minutes or until tomatoes begin to burst, stirring after 3 minutes.
4. Crush tomatoes using the back of a spoon.
5. Add pasta, broth, salt, and black pepper.
6. Return baker (or casserole dish) to microwave; cover and microwave on HIGH for 18-20 minutes or until pasta is tender, stirring after 15 minutes.
7. Carefully remove the baker from the microwave and remove the lid, lifting away from you.
8. Add cheese and chicken to the baker; mix well. Add basil and mix well.

Toast Nuts in The Microwave

If you're looking for a quick and easy snack, toast some nuts in the microwave. All you need is a microwave-safe dish and a handful of your favorite nuts. Place the nuts in the dish and cook on high for 1-2 minutes, stirring occasionally. Enjoy your warm, toasty nuts, plain or with a little salt or sugar.

PREP TIME 3 minutes | COOK TIME 5 minutes | TOTAL TIME 8 minutes

Ingredients

- ✓ 2 cups whole walnuts or your desired nuts
- ✓ 1 teaspoon vegetable oil
- ✓ fine sea salt (optional)

Instructions

1. Toss one cup of nuts with vegetable oil. Spread the oiled nuts out in a single layer on a microwave-safe plate.
2. Toast in one-minute intervals, stirring between each interval. One cup of nuts can take anywhere from 5 to 10 minutes overall, depending on the quantity and size of the nuts used.
3. To make salted nuts: Toss toasted nuts with fine sea salt to taste.

Crispy Microwave Bacon

Bacon is a delicious breakfast treat, but many people avoid it because of the greasy mess it leaves behind. Cooking bacon in the microwave is a great way to enjoy it without the hassle. Just place a few strips of bacon on a paper towel-lined plate and microwave for 3-4 minutes. The bacon will be crispy and delicious, with no cleanup required!

Prep Time 7 minutes | Cook Time 6 minutes | Total Time 13 minutes

Ingredients

- ✓ 10 oz bacon (2 packages, 10 medium-thick slices)

Instructions

1. Place two paper towels on a microwave-safe dinner plate.
2. Arrange four slices of bacon on the paper towels, not touching each other.
3. Place two more paper towels on top of the bacon slices.
4. Microwave on high until crispy. In my microwave, this takes 4 minutes.
5. Remove the plate carefully from the microwave. It will be very hot.
6. Repeat with the four remaining slices.

Microwave Peanut Brittle

When it comes to making peanut brittle, the microwave is your best friend. This quick and easy recipe will have you feeling like a candy-making pro in no time. And with just a few simple ingredients, you can indulge in this sweet and salty treat any time the craving hits. So, let's get started!

Prep time 25 minutes | Cooking time 15 minutes

Ingredients

- ✓ 2 cups white sugar
- ✓ 1 cup light corn syrup
- ✓ 2 cups salted peanuts
- ✓ 2 teaspoons butter
- ✓ 2 teaspoons vanilla extract
- ✓ 2 teaspoons baking soda

Directions

1. Grease your cookie sheet with butter.
2. In a 3-quart glass bowl, combine sugar and corn syrup. Microwave for 5 minutes on high.
3. Stir in peanuts and microwave on high for another 5 minutes. Stir in butter and vanilla. Microwave for 3 minutes and 35 seconds.
4. Stir in baking soda until the batter becomes light and foamy. Pour batter onto the cookie sheet. Spread so that it's even and thin.
5. Cool completely and break into pieces.
6. Enjoy!

Cinnamon Roll in a Mug

This single-serve recipe is the perfect solution when you don't have the time to make a whole cinnamon roll from scratch. Made in a mug and cooked in the microwave, this cinnamon roll can be ready in just a few minutes. And since it's made with just a few simple ingredients, you likely already have everything you need on hand. So, give this recipe a try the next time you're craving a cinnamon roll but don't want to make an entire batch.

Ingredients

Dough

- ✓ 2 tablespoons salted butter, melted (set aside)
- ✓ 1 cup all-purpose flour
- ✓ 1 teaspoon baking powder
- ✓ 3 tablespoons granulated sugar
- ✓ 4 tablespoons milk. I prefer whole milk
- ✓ 1 teaspoon vanilla

Filling

- ✓ 2 tablespoons butter
- ✓ 3 tablespoons brown sugar
- ✓ 1 teaspoon cinnamon

Glaze

- ✓ 2/3 cup confectioners' sugar
- ✓ 1 tablespoon milk (can also use heavy cream)

Instructions

Dough

1. Add the flour, baking powder, granulated sugar, milk, vanilla, and melted butter to a small bowl and stir until combined.
2. Once the dough is solid, drop it onto a clean and lightly floured surface.

3. Use your hands to flatten the dough into a rectangle.

Filling

Melt the butter, brown sugar, and cinnamon in a small bowl for about 5 minutes. (Depending on how cold your butter is.) Stir well.

Assembly

1. Pour filling over the dough rectangle and roll up into a cinnamon roll shape.
2. Place roll into a mug (I prefer to use a standard-size mug, nothing too wide). Make sure your mug is sprayed with non-stick spray or greased.
3. Heat in the microwave for 95 seconds. If the roll remains wet on top, select 15-second increments. If the roll appears dry, the cinnamon roll is done. You can also employ a toothpick to check.

Glaze

1. Stir confectioners sugar and milk together in a bowl until smooth.
2. Pour over the warm cinnamon roll in the mug or invert the roll onto a plate and pour glaze over the top.

Macaroni and Cheese in a Mug

You can have a hot, cheesy mug of macaroni and cheese in just a few minutes, satisfying your comfort food cravings. This recipe is easy to follow and only requires a few ingredients you probably already have in your pantry. With a microwave and a mug, you can have a delicious single serving of mac and cheese that will hit the spot.

Prep Time: 3 minutes | Cook Time: 5 minutes | Total Time: 8 minutes

Ingredients

- ✓ 1 cup small elbow macaroni
- ✓ 1 cup water
- ✓ 1 cup finely shredded cheddar cheese
- ✓ salt and pepper or hot sauce is optional; it adds more flavor

Instructions

1. Add water and macaroni into an extra large mug (I recommend at least a 30-ounce mug/2.5 cups). Place the mug on a large plate (this is to catch the overflow of water that occurs when cooking). Your macaroni should only rise to 2/3 or at least 1 of the mug. Microwave at full power for 3 minutes. Remove the mug and stir the macaroni, making sure to loosen any macaroni that may be stuck to the bottom of the mug.
2. Microwave for an additional 3 minutes and stir again. During this 2nd minute is when the water tends to overflow a little. If it's only a little water, then it should be fine. If it's a lot of water, you may need to add a little water to your macaroni later. Macaroni should be almost cooked after the 2nd-minute mark. The most liquid should be almost gone, but your macaroni should still be moist. How much more you need to cook will depend on your microwave.
3. Continue to cook the macaroni at 35-second intervals, stirring in between. If your macaroni gets very dry, add 1 tbsp of water. However, adding water will increase cooking time, so you only need to add water if your macaroni is dry. If it's moist but not watery, do not add more water. The microwave will cook the moist

macaroni. After the first 30 seconds, my macaroni was cooked but still al dente. Almost all the water was evaporated though the pasta was still very moist. I then microwaved for 35 more seconds. At this point, my noodles were completely cooked and soft and no water remained. My macaroni was cooked for a total of 5 minutes.

4. Stirring rapidly to add cheese to the macaroni, cook until the cheese has completely melted and evenly mingled with the mac 'n' cheese. Cook a little longer to add more salt, ground black pepper, or hot sauce. Counsel everyone to eat immediately.

Microwave Peanut Butter Fudge

If you're looking for an easy, no-fail fudge recipe that can be made in the microwave in just a few minutes, this is the one for you! Peanut butter fudge is a classic flavor everyone loves, and this recipe adds a little bit of sea salt to give it a little extra flavor. You'll be amazed at how simple this recipe is to make and how delicious it turns out.

Prep time 5 minutes | Cooking time 3 minutes

Ingredients

- ✓ 10 oz unsalted butter
- ✓ 2 cups creamy peanut butter
- ✓ 4-pound powdered sugar

Instructions

1. Line an 8x8 inch pan with parchment paper. Use enough so that the paper hangs over the side. This makes it much easier to remove the fudge from the pan.
2. In a microwave-safe bowl, combine butter and peanut butter. Microwave for 1 minute and stir. Microwave for another minute and stir until mixture is completely smooth and incorporated.
3. Add in the powdered sugar and stir until smooth. You'll know it's done when you see a thick, paste-like batter.
4. Spread the batter onto the lined baking pan. Place a sheet of parchment paper on top of the fudge and start pressing with your palms to spread evenly across the pan.
5. Refrigerate for at least 2.30 hours. Remove the fudge from the pan and cut into small, 1-inch squares using a sharp knife.
6. Enjoy!

Microwave Apples with Cinnamon

When it comes to Fall desserts, apple pie is king. But who has the time to make a whole pie when craving something sweet? This single-serve microwave apple with the cinnamon recipe is the perfect solution. In just 5 minutes, you can have a warm, comforting dessert that satisfies your sweet tooth. So go ahead and indulge - your secret is safe with us!

PREP TIME 5 mins | COOK TIME 3 mins | TOTAL TIME 8 mins

Ingredients

- ✓ 2 small apples - Golden Delicious or Granny Smith are my favorites
- ✓ 2 packets of sweetener - Stevia is my favorite or a teaspoon of sugar
- ✓ 3/4 teaspoon cinnamon
- ✓ 3/4 teaspoon cornstarch
- ✓ 2 tablespoons water

Instructions

1. Peel or don't peel an apple, core, and slice or dice. Place in the freezer-quality plastic zippered bag along with the remaining ingredients.
2. Seal the plastic bag and shake well to mix the ingredients. (If you prefer, place all ingredients into a small microwave-safe bowl and cover loosely.)
3. Reopen the bag with just a touch to vent. Microwave on High for 3 minutes-- longer if you use a big apple.
4. Carefully (it will be HOT and steamy) open the bag and pour over plain or cinnamon-sugar pita chips, flour tortilla chips, oatmeal, or ice cream.

Microwave Mug Pizza

A microwave mug is a personal pizza you can make in a mug in the microwave. It's a quick and easy way to satisfy your pizza craving without having to order delivery or make a whole pie. All you need is a mug, pizza dough, sauce, and toppings. You can have a fresh and hot pizza all to yourself in just a few minutes.

Prep Time 7 mins | Cook Time 3 mins | Total Time 10 mins

Ingredients

- ✓ 5 tablespoons all-purpose flour
- ✓ 3/8 teaspoon baking powder
- ✓ 5/16 teaspoon baking soda
- ✓ 3/8 teaspoon salt
- ✓ 4 tablespoons milk
- ✓ 2 tablespoons olive oil
- ✓ 2 tablespoons marinara sauce
- ✓ 2 generous tablespoons shredded mozzarella cheese
- ✓ 7 mini pepperonis
- ✓ 1 teaspoon dried Italian herbs (basil or oregano will work)

Instructions

1. Mix the flour, baking powder, soda, and salt in a microwavable mug.
2. Add in the milk and oil, then mix together. There might be some lumps, but that is ok.
3. Spoon on the marinara sauce and spread it around the surface of the batter.
4. Sprinkle on the cheese, pepperoni, and dried herbs
5. Microwave for 3 minutes 14 - 3 minutes 25 seconds, or until it rises up and the toppings are bubbling (timing is based on my 1250W microwave, so your timing might vary)
6. Enjoy straight away!

Microwave Caramel Popcorn

Microwave caramel popcorn is a delicious and easy snack to make at home. It only takes a few minutes to prepare, and it's a great way to satisfy your sweet tooth. This recipe is perfect for anyone who loves caramel popcorn but doesn't want to deal with the hassle of making it from scratch.

Prep time 7 minutes | Cooking time 15 minutes

Ingredients

- ✓ 5 quarters cooked popcorn
- ✓ 2 cups brown sugar
- ✓ 1 cup butter or margarine
- ✓ 3/4 cup light corn syrup
- ✓ 1 teaspoon salt
- ✓ 2 teaspoons vanilla extract
- ✓ 1 teaspoon baking soda

Directions

1. Place the popped popcorn in a large brown paper bag.
2. In a 2-quart casserole or heat-proof glass dish, stir the brown sugar, margarine, corn syrup, salt, and vanilla until combined. Heat in the microwave for 5 minutes at 3-minute intervals, stirring well in between. Stir in the baking soda until combined.
3. Pour the syrup over the popcorn and seal the bag by rolling the top once or twice. Give the bag a good shake to coat the popcorn with the syrup.
4. Place the bag in the microwave and cook on high powder for 1 minute and 15 seconds. Shake the bag vigorously and microwave for another 1 minute and 15 seconds. Transfer the popcorn onto a piece of parchment or wax paper. Let the coated popcorn cool and set. Enjoy!

Microwave Granola in a Mug

Granola is a healthy and delicious snack that can be enjoyed by everyone. Even better, it can be made in a microwave in just a few minutes! This recipe is perfect for those mornings when you don't have time to make breakfast or for an afternoon snack. Just grab a mug, add your ingredients, and zap it in the microwave. You'll have a warm, tasty, and nutritious treat in no time!

Prep Time 7 mins | Cook Time 5 mins | Total Time 12 mins

Ingredients

- ✓ 2 tablespoons maple syrup (honey or agave)
- ✓ 3 teaspoons water
- ✓ 3 teaspoons vegetable oil
- ✓ 3/8 teaspoons salt
- ✓ 5 tablespoons rolled oats
- ✓ 2 tablespoons desiccated coconut
- ✓ 2 tablespoons pecans, chopped

Instructions

1. Mix the maple syrup, water, oil, salt, oats, and nuts in the large microwave-safe mug until blended.
2. Microwave for 3 minutes 35 seconds and stir, stirring up any syrup on the bottom of the mug. (Timing is based on my 1200W microwave, so your timing might vary)
3. Microwave for 3 minutes longer or until oats is golden brown. You will see them getting golden in color and starting to toast up. Be careful it doesn't get too hot as it can burn.
4. Let it stand for 3 to 5 minutes to cool before eating. If you have an extra, store it in an airtight container for 5 days.

Easy Microwave Cauliflower

This cauliflower dish is easy to make and requires only a few ingredients. You can have it on the table in less than 30 minutes, and it's a great healthy alternative to other side dishes.

Prep Time 7 minutes | Cook Time 13 minutes | Total Time 20 minutes

Ingredients

- ✓ 2 medium head cauliflowers (2 lb. whole, 1 lb. without refuse)
- ✓ 2 tablespoons olive oil
- ✓ 2 tablespoons freshly squeezed lemon juice
- ✓ 1 teaspoon Diamond Crystal kosher salt
- ✓ 3/4 teaspoon freshly ground black pepper

Instructions

1. Wash and trim the cauliflower. Cut it into florets.
2. Place the cauliflower florets in a large microwave-safe bowl. Add ¼ cup of cold water to the bowl.
3. Cover the bowl tightly with a microwave-safe plate or plastic wrap (not touching the cauliflower).
4. Microwave on high for about 15 minutes until the cauliflower is tender-crisp. Use oven mitts when removing the bowl from the microwave, place it on a trivet, and be careful when removing the plate or the cling wrap. The bowl will be very hot, and the hot steam will escape.
5. If desired, season the cauliflower with salt, pepper, lemon juice, and olive oil. Serve immediately.

Microwave a Sweet Potato

When it comes to cooking a sweet potato, several methods can be used. One popular method is to microwave the sweet potato. This method is quick and easy, producing delicious and healthy results. Here are some tips on how to microwave a sweet potato.

Prep Time 6 minutes | Cook Time 9 minutes | Total Time 15 minutes

Ingredients

- ✓ 2 sweet potatoes

Toppings:

- ✓ Salt and pepper to taste
- ✓ 2 tablespoons butter
- ✓ 2 teaspoons brown sugar
- ✓ Ground cinnamon

Instructions

1. Wash the sweet potato thoroughly, pat dry, and pierce 4-5 times with a fork.
2. Place on a microwave-safe plate and microwave for 6 minutes. If the potato isn't fork-tender after 6 minutes, continue microwaving in 3-minute increments until ready.
3. Slice potato in half lengthwise, season with salt, pepper, a sprinkle of brown sugar, and top with 2 tablespoons of butter.
4. Sprinkle with ground cinnamon and serve.

Microwave Fantasy Fudge

If you're looking for a delicious, quick, and easy dessert, look no further than this Microwave Fantasy Fudge. Made with just a few simple ingredients, this fudge is rich, creamy, and will satisfy your sweet tooth. In just minutes, you can have a batch of this delicious fudge to share with friends and family.

Prep time 15 minutes | Cooking time 15 minutes

Ingredients

- ✓ 4 cups white sugar
- ✓ 1 cup margarine
- ✓ 1 cup evaporated milk
- ✓ 2 (22 oz) packages of semi-sweet chocolate chips
- ✓ 2 (10 oz) jar marshmallow creme
- ✓ 2 cups chopped walnuts
- ✓ 2 teaspoons vanilla extract

Instructions

1. Grease a 9x13-inch pan.
2. Place margarine in a 4-quart microwave-safe dish and microwave until it melts. Mix in sugar and milk until combined.
3. Microwave the mixture for 7 minutes on high or until it begins to boil. Stir the mixture after 5 minutes, ensuring that the sides of the bowl are scraped well. Microwave the mixture for 6 1/2 more minutes.
4. Remove from microwave and stir in the chocolate chips until melted. Add in the marshmallow creme, walnuts, and vanilla extract. Mix well.
5. Pour the fudge into the 9x13 inch baking pan. Let the fudge cool and then cut into squares.
6. Enjoy!

Oreo Mug Cake

You can enjoy a delicious Oreo mug cake in just a few minutes! This treat is perfect for satisfying your sweet tooth without making a big mess. All you need is a mug, a few ingredients, and a microwave. This recipe is so simple and quick that you'll make it again and again!

Prep Time 3 min | Total Time 3 mins

Ingredients

- ✓ 7 tbsp milk
- ✓ 3 tbsp oil
- ✓ 3/4 cup flour
- ✓ 3 tbsp unsweetened cocoa powder
- ✓ 3 tbsp sugar
- ✓ 3 Oreos lightly crushed, plus extra to top
- ✓ 3/4 tsp baking powder
- ✓ 2 pinch salt
- ✓ 2 tbsp chocolate chips or chopped chocolate

Instructions

1. In a large mug, whisk together the milk and oil.
2. Mix the flour, cocoa, crushed Oreos, sugar, baking powder, and salt in a small bowl.
3. Add the flour mix to the mug and mix well until there are no lumps.
4. Sprinkle on the chocolate and extra crushed Oreos if using.
5. Place on a microwave-safe plate and microwave for 2 minutes and 25 seconds.
6. Let cool slightly and enjoy!

Pancake In a Mug

In today's busy world, it's hard to find time to make a homemade breakfast. However, with this pancake-in-a-mug recipe, you can have a delicious and nutritious breakfast in just minutes! This recipe is perfect for those mornings you need to grab and go. All you need is a mug, a few simple ingredients, and a microwave. You can enjoy a hot and fluffy pancake topped with your favorite fruit or syrup in just a few minutes.

Prep Time: 2 min | Cook Time: 2 min | Total Time: 4 mins

Ingredients

- ✓ 3/4 cup flour
- ✓ 2 tsp sugar
- ✓ 1 tsp baking powder
- ✓ 4 tbsp milk or water. I like to use milk
- ✓ 1 tsp vanilla

Instructions

1. In a microwave-safe mug, combine flour, sugar, and baking powder.
2. Add in vanilla and milk or water, mixing well.
3. Microwave for 65 seconds.
4. Remove from the microwave and top with the desired topping, such as maple syrup, honey, no added sugar, blueberry jam, yogurt, etc.!

Microwave a Potato

A potato is a starchy tuber that is a staple food in many parts of the world. It can be cooked in various ways, including baking, boiling, and frying. Microwaving is a quick and convenient way to cook a potato. This method is suitable for small or medium-sized potatoes. To microwave a potato, start by scrubbing it clean and pricking it several times with a fork.

Prep Time 7 minutes | Cook Time 15 minutes | Total Time 22 minutes

Ingredients

- ✓ 2 large russet potatoes
- ✓ 2 tablespoons butter
- ✓ 4 tablespoons shredded Cheddar cheese
- ✓ salt and pepper to taste
- ✓ 2 tablespoons sour cream
- ✓ Chopped green onions

Instructions

1. Scrub and wash the potato well. Prick several times with a fork. Place on a plate.
2. Cook on full power in the microwave for 7 minutes. Turn over and cook for another 7 more minutes.
3. When the potato is soft, remove it from the microwave, and cut it in half lengthwise.
4. Season with salt and pepper, and mash the inside with a fork. Top with butter and cheese. Return to the microwave and cook for 1 minute to melt the cheese.
5. Top with sour cream and green onions and serve.

Printed in Great Britain
by Amazon